21st Century Skills INNOVATION Library

Video Gaming

by Trudi Strain Trueit

Published in the United States of America by Cherry Lake Publishing
Ann Arbor, Michigan
www.cherrylakepublishing.com

Content Adviser: Victor B. Zordan, PhD, Assistant Professor, University of California, Riverside

Design: The Design Lab

Photo Credits: Cover and page 3, ©AP Photo/Shizuo Kambayashi, FILE; page 4, ©Blend Images/Alamy; page 6, ©AP Photo/The Journal Record, Jennifer Pitts; page 8, ©iStockphoto.com/webphotographeer; page 11, ©AP Photo/Mike Derer; page 12, ©iStockphoto.com/AzureLaRoux; page 13, ©ArcadeImages/Alamy; page 15, ©Jamaway/Alamy; page 17, ©AP Photo/Marcio Jose Sanchez; page 19, ©AP Photo/Jakub Mosur; page 21, ©AP Photo/Ric Francis; page 22, ©AP Photo/The Nashville Tennessean, Steven Harman; page 25, ©AP Photo/Pablo Martinez Monsivais; page 27, ©jeremy sutton-hibbert/Alamy; page 28, ©Jenny Matthews/Alamy; page 32, ©Bill Trueit

Library of Congress Cataloging-in-Publication Data
Trueit, Trudi Strain.
Video gaming / by Trudi Strain Trueit.
p. cm.—(Innovation in entertainment)
Includes index.
ISBN-13: 978-1-60279-218-0
ISBN-10: 1-60279-218-6
1. Video games—Juvenile literature. I. Title. II. Series.
GV1469.3.T78 2009
794.8—dc22 2008014184

Cherry Lake Publishing would like to acknowledge the work of The Partnership for 21st Century Skills. Please visit www.21stcenturyskills.org *for more information.*

CONTENTS

CHAPTER ONE

Let the Games Begin

Video games can be played alone or with friends.

Did you know the average kid in the United States plays video games for about an hour each day? Video games are part of American culture. They teach us. They entertain us. You can play lead guitar in a rock band, battle dragons in an ancient land, or become an Olympic snowboarding champion—all without leaving home. But it wasn't always this way. Video games got their start about 50 years ago with very basic games and very big computers.

American scientist William Higinbotham created one of the earliest computer games. In 1958, the U.S. government research center he worked for was planning an open house. Higinbotham thought visitors might enjoy a game. He opened a computer manual to a page that showed how to create a program for a curve like the one a bouncing ball makes. That was it! Higinbotham decided to create a tennis game. He ran *Tennis for Two* on an **oscilloscope**. An oscilloscope is a device that shows electrical currents on a screen. In his tennis game, a dot represented the ball, and a vertical line represented the net. The concept was simple: players used knobs to send the ball across the net. The screen was just 5 inches (12.7 centimeters) wide. At the open house, *Tennis for Two* was a smash hit.

A few years later, a college student named Steve Russell was experimenting with a new computer at the Massachusetts Institute of Technology. At the time, computers were huge. A single computer could fill a room! The Programmed Data Processor-1, or PDP-1, was the size of a car. This "mini" computer, as it was considered then, also came with a screen. Back then, most computers didn't have screens or monitors. Instead, the computers gave printed readouts. Russell wrote a game program for the PDP-1 called *Spacewar!* In the game, two players flew rockets around a starry sky, firing

Nolan Bushnell is an innovator who knows how to take an idea and turn it into a successful product.

missiles at each other. Russell thought about selling *Spacewar!* but knew only certain computers could run it. So he gave it away.

Soon *Spacewar!* was popping up on university computers across the country. In 1965, it caught the eye of Nolan Bushnell. He was an engineering student in Utah. Bushnell worked part-time at an amusement park arcade. At the time, arcades had target shooting galleries and pinball machines. Bushnell thought it would be great if they had computer games, too. But computers were big

Two girls play a *Pong* arcade game at an exhibit tracing the development of video games.

The Famicom was renamed Nintendo Entertainment System, or NES, for its release in the United States. When it hit the market in 1985, sales took off. Nintendo sold more than 60 million NES units worldwide and forever changed the home video game market.

While on a train one day, Yokoi noticed that people were playing with their calculators to pass the time. It sparked an idea for creating portable games. This would allow people to play video games wherever they wanted. In 1989, Yokoi's team released Game Boy. It was a handheld video game with interchangeable cartridges. It wasn't the only portable game on the market. But it could last far longer on battery power than its competitors. Over the years, games such as *The Legend of Zelda* and *Pokémon* helped Nintendo sell more than 150 million Game Boys worldwide.

Game Boy and other portable gaming systems allow gamers to play anywhere.

CHAPTER THREE

Minds at Play

Did you ever wonder where game designers get their ideas? One of the earliest hit video games came from an exam used to test the skills of computer programmers. Japanese gamemaker Taito decided to turn the test into an arcade video game. In 1978, *Space Invaders* was released. It was the first video game to have animated characters and a high-score tally. At one point, people in Japan were plugging so

Space Invaders was one of the first big arcade video hits.

Learning & Innovation Skills

In 1979, Japanese game-designer Toru Iwatani set out to invent something different. At the time, the most common options available to players were shooting games. When Iwatani overheard a group of girls in a café talking about food, he thought a game about eating might be just the thing.

Iwatani likes to say he ordered a pizza for lunch, lifted out a slice, "and there it was, the figure of Pac-Man." Soon Iwatani and his designers had Pac-Man gobbling up dots, fruit, and power pills while scurrying through a maze. By acting on a simple but creative idea, Iwatani helped create a pop culture phenomenon. There were Pac-Man clothes, watches, lunch boxes, and even a Saturday morning cartoon. The makers of *Pac-Man* estimate the arcade version of the game has been played more than 10 billion times!

much money into *Space Invaders* it caused a nationwide shortage of coins!

In 1980, Atari released the tank warfare game *Battlezone*. It featured some of the first **three-dimensional**, or 3-D, images ever seen in a video game. Instead of being flat, objects had depth. *Battlezone* was revolutionary in another way, too. It put the player in the driver's seat of a tank. Gamers loved the new perspective, which became known as first-person shooter. The U.S. Army even requested a special version of *Battlezone* to use for training. But Ed Rotberg, the game's main programmer, wasn't pleased by the request. He wanted the game to remain just that—a game.

Artist Shigeru Miyamoto was designing toys for Nintendo when his boss asked him to develop an arcade game to be sold in the United States. He created a story

Super Mario Brothers is one of the best selling video game series of all time.

about a gorilla escaping from its owner, a carpenter named Jumpman. Miyamoto planned on naming the game *Stubborn Gorilla*. He picked up a Japanese-English dictionary to help him translate the title. He chose the word *donkey* for stubborn and the word *kong* for gorilla and named the game *Donkey Kong*. A few years later, Miyamoto redesigned the game. He changed Jumpman's name after Nintendo employees in America pointed out that the hero looked a lot like their warehouse manager,

Mario. *Mario Brothers*, *Super Mario Brothers*, and their many spin-offs remain among Nintendo's biggest-selling games.

As a child, Will Wright dreamed of being an astronaut. He wanted to help establish human colonies in space to handle overpopulation on Earth. Though his career didn't take him in that direction, he has helped create many new civilizations here on Earth. Well, sort of. In 1989, Wright turned the gaming world upside down with *SimCity* (short for Simulated City). The computer video game had no violence, no aliens, and no ending. Instead, players learned about the real world as they built and ran a virtual city. It took a while for people to catch on, but once they did, it started a new trend in reality gaming. Released in 2000, *The Sims* became one of the top-selling PC games of all time. Gamers can now play *The Sims* online.

Now that you know how video game designers are inspired, read on to discover what it takes to turn a good idea into a hit game.

CHAPTER FOUR

From Start to Sell

What is one of the most popular forms of entertainment in the United States? If you said video gaming, you're right. In 2007, video game sales reached nearly $18 billion. That's even more popular than the movies. In the early days, a small group of people

Will Wright (above) created the best-selling *The Sims* games. As of April 2008, 100 million copies of the games had been sold.

could create a successful video game. Not anymore. Fierce competition for your gaming dollars has companies trying to top each other. Developing a single video game now takes hundreds of artists, writers, and programmers, and may cost millions of dollars! Companies are always trying to find the next big thing in video games.

Once an idea for a video game is chosen, writers and artists come up with a **storyboard**. This is a series of drawings done in comic book style. Storyboards show what will occur in each scene. Because a game may go in hundreds, or thousands, of different directions, artists must sketch out many possible outcomes. Once the storyboard is finished, a final drawing of each character can be scanned into a computer to be turned into a three-dimensional figure.

Now it is time to make the characters come to life. Voice tracks, sound effects, and music are added. Programmers then write the code, a set of computer language instructions. The code is the logic of the game. It determines what the characters will say and do, and how the game will progress. The designer may also add **Easter eggs**. These are hidden surprises for players to find. In the late 1970s, Atari game designer Warren Robinett created the first Easter egg. It was for his game *Adventure*. In *Adventure*, discovering a tiny dot that blended in with the background led to a secret room. It

Artists create storyboards for video games and other forms of entertainment. Here an artist works on a storyboard for a children's cartoon.

was only after Atari sold thousands of the games that a 12-year-old boy in Salt Lake City, Utah, discovered the room. It caused a media frenzy. Today, serious gamers expect, and carefully search for, cleverly planted Easter eggs.

21st Century Content

In the 1990s, extremely violent video games such as *Doom* and *Mortal Kombat* sparked debate over the effect these kinds of games had on children. Some game designers argued that violent games had little impact. They said that gamers understood the difference between reality and gaming. Many lawmakers and citizens weren't so sure, especially after several school shootings. In some cases, the teen criminals were also fans of violent video games. In 2005, Senators Hillary Clinton and Joe Lieberman introduced the Family Entertainment Protection Act. It would have prevented children from buying games rated "Mature" and "Adults Only." The bill never became law.

What do you think? Do violent video games influence behavior? Should there be tighter restrictions on who can buy certain video games? Why or why not?

A video game goes through several levels of testing before it is ready to be sold to the public. Testers must play the game hundreds of times to find any errors, or **bugs**, in the system. During testing, a copy of the game is usually sent to the Entertainment Software Rating Board, or ESRB. The board assigns each video game one of six ratings. These are: Early Childhood (EC), Everyone (E), Everyone 10 and older (E10+), Teen (T), Mature (M), and Adults Only (AO).

After the testing and rating phases are complete, the game is ready to be manufactured, packaged, and released. A good marketing plan is important. Sales teams spend months crafting big-budget television commercials, theatrical trailers, and Internet ads. They go to conventions and trade shows to

Video game manufacturers send sales teams to conventions to help spread the word about new products.

demonstrate the new game. It's not uncommon to spend $10 million to $20 million to promote a game. That's not much when you consider that a hit game can bring in hundreds of millions of dollars. In less than three years, Activision's *Guitar Hero* series earned $1 billion in North America alone!

Today, the ever-growing popularity of video gaming keeps companies such as Nintendo, Sony, Sega, and Microsoft on the cutting edge of gaming technology.

Games such as *Guitar Hero* are popular with people of all ages.

Game consoles now offer the latest in high-definition images, Internet connection, wireless controllers, and motion sensors. Nintendo's Wii system uses wireless controls. It's designed to make players feel like part of the action. Holding the controller, players can pretend to putt a golf ball, swing a tennis racket, or even knock out an opponent in the boxing ring.

Improvements in wireless technology may someday allow you to buy a game console without any wires at all. Or how about playing a game using only your thoughts? Believe it or not, it's already happening. *Play Attention* is an educational game by Unique Logic and Technology. It helps students with **attention-deficit/hyperactivity disorder** (ADHD) learn to focus. Players wear a special helmet that detects brain waves. If you think of flying, the airplane on the screen takes off! Who knows what the next wave of video games may bring? Whatever the future holds, you can be sure that a nation of die-hard gamers will be ready to play.

CHAPTER FIVE

They've Got Game

In the fast-paced world of video games, it takes originality, hard work, and a bit of luck to succeed. A few people stand out as especially important innovators who have put their creative spin on the games we play.

Video Game Visionary

At age 16, Ralph Baer left Germany and came to the United States. He went on to complete one of the first college programs for television engineering offered in the United States. Baer became a pioneer in the video game industry. He invented the first home video game console for television. He also created hit games like *Simon*, *Maniac*, and *Computer Perfection*. In 2005, Baer donated his original TV game units to the Smithsonian Institution in Washington DC.

Ralph Baer (left) receives the National Medal o
Technology from President Bush in 2006.

Life & Career Skills

In 1980, Dona Bailey joined Atari. She was the only female software designer among a group of 30 men. Bailey co-created *Centipede*. It was a hit arcade game that revolutionized the industry with its use of artificial intelligence.

Some people refused to believe a woman was capable of such groundbreaking work!

Bailey would not have been able to succeed unless she could work productively with others. Even when faced with criticism, she stayed committed to achieving her goal. Bailey helped blaze the trail for women in the gaming industry. Even so, currently, only about one in 10 video game designers is a woman. Have you ever been in a situation where you felt you had to prove yourself? What did you do?

Master of the Game

Gunpei Yokoi's passion for electronic gadgets started when he was a child in Kyoto, Japan. After graduating from college with a degree in electronics, he joined Nintendo. Back then, the game company made playing cards. In his spare time, Yokoi designed and made toys. His bosses took notice. Eventually, Nintendo moved into the electronic age, and Yokoi took a leadership role. He was the force behind mega-selling products such as the NES console and the Game Boy. He also helped introduce the world to games such as *Donkey Kong*, *Mario Brothers*, and the *Metroid* series.

Pokémon Phenomenon

Growing up outside of Tokyo, Satoshi Tajiri suffered from Asperger's syndrome. The disorder makes it hard for a person to interact with others. He

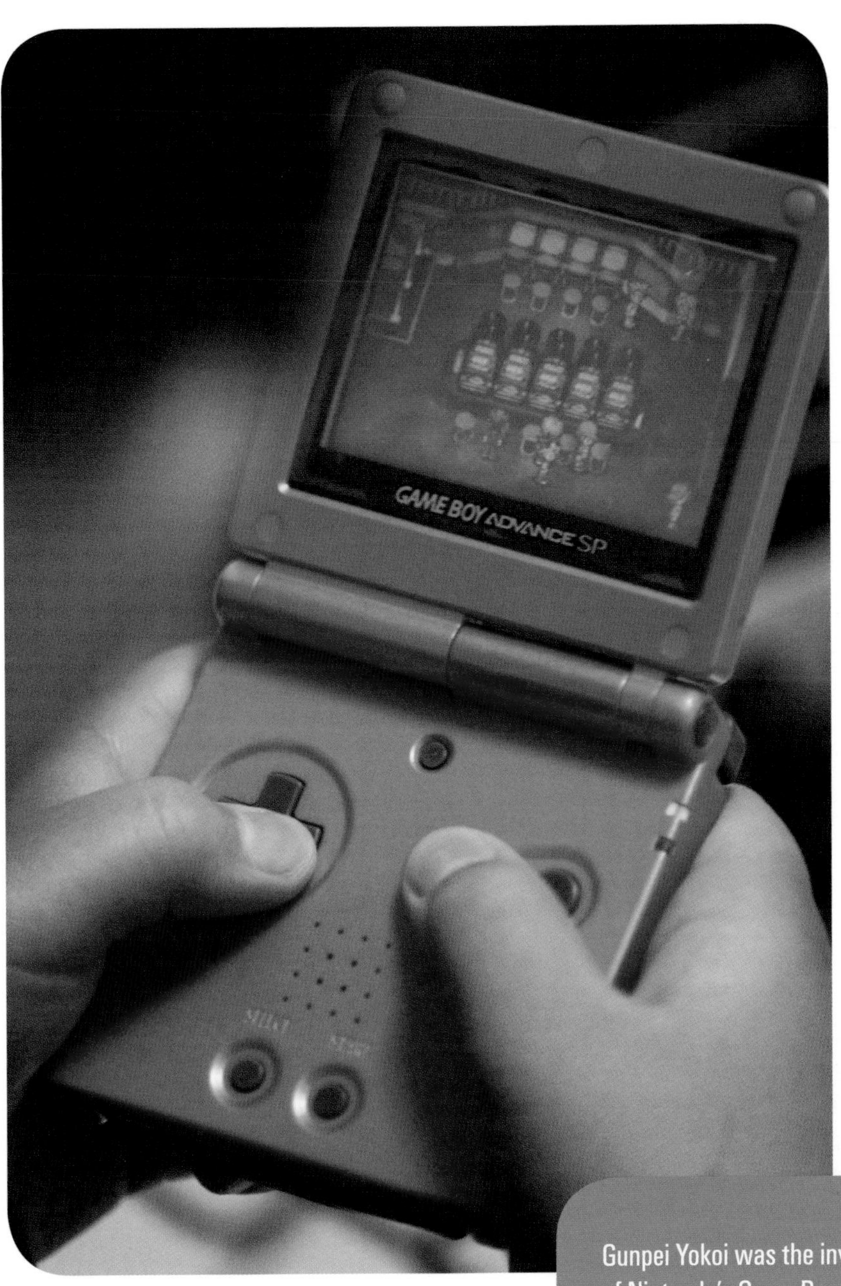

Gunpei Yokoi was the inventor behind the success of Nintendo's Game Boy system.

loved playing video games at the local arcade. When he was 17, Tajiri and a couple of friends created a gaming magazine. It was called *Game Freak*. His friend drew the pocket monsters, or pokémon, while Tajiri wrote the

Pokémon trading cards are just one successful product that features the popular pocket monsters.

articles. The handmade magazines sold more than 10,000 copies. In 1991, Tajiri sold his first video game, *Quinty*, to Nintendo. But it was Game Boy that changed his life. Tajiri thought a game where players captured pocket monsters would be a perfect fit for the portable system. It was! In 1998, Nintendo released *Pokémon* in the United States. It sold a million copies in the first month. *Pokémon* trading cards, cartoons, and movies, along with many variations of the game followed. An empire was born.

Glossary

attention-deficit/hyperactivity disorder (uh-TEN-shuhn-DEF-uh-sit hye-pur-ack-TIV-uh-tee dis-OR-dur) a condition which makes it difficult for a person to pay attention and to control his or her impulses

bugs (BUHGZ) errors in the design of a video game or computer program that prevent it from working properly

Easter eggs (EE-stur EGZ) hidden surprises or features programmed into a game

joystick (JOI-stik) a handheld lever used to control movement in a video game or computer game

microchip (MYE-kroh-chip) a thin piece of material such as silicon that has electronic circuits printed on it

oscilloscope (ah-SIL-uh-skohp) a device that displays electrical current

patent (PAT-ent) a legal document that gives only one person or group permission to make or sell an item

prototype (PROH-tuh-tipe) an original model of an invention

storyboard (STOR-ee-bord) a series of sketches that shows what will occur in each scene of a video game

three-dimensional (three-duh-MEN-shuh-nuhl) having, or appearing to have, depth

For More Information

BOOKS

Bancroft, Tom. *Creating Characters with Personality*. New York: Watson-Guptill, 2006.

Cohen, Judith Love. *You Can Be a Woman Video Game Producer*. Marina del Rey, CA: Cascade Pass, 2005.

Hodgson, David S. J., Bryan Stratton, and Alice Rush. *Paid to Play: An Insider's Guide to Video Game Careers*. Roseville, CA: Prima, 2006.

WEB SITES

Twin Galaxies
www.twingalaxies.com
Learn more about the world's top video gamers at this electronic scoreboard site featuring player profiles and the latest gaming news

The Video Game Revolution
www.pbs.org/kcts/videogamerevolution
Explore the history of video games, take a quiz, and play classic video games

Women in Games International
www.womeningamesinternational.org
Founded in 2005, this nonprofit organization encourages girls and women to seek careers in the video gaming industry

Index

About the Author

Trudi Strain Trueit spent much of her childhood in Seattle, Washington, playing *Pac-Man* and *Breakout*—after doing her homework, of course. She earned her college degree in broadcast journalism and spent several years as a television news reporter. Now a freelance writer, Ms. Trueit has published more than 40 fiction and nonfiction books for children, including the Innovation Library title *Animation*. She still makes her home near Seattle with her husband, Bill. And she still loves classic video games. You'll often find her playing *Q*bert*, after she's finished writing for the day. Read more about Trudi and her books at www.truditrueit.com.